BUILT FOR SUCCESS

THE STORY OF

Google

First published in the UK in 2013 by
Franklin Watts
338 Euston Road
London NW1 3BH

Franklin Watts Australia
Level 17/207 Kent Street
Sydney, NSW 2000

First published by Creative Education, an imprint of
The Creative Company.
www.thecreativecompany.us

A CIP catalogue record for this book is available from the
British Library.

ISBN: 978 1 4451 2097 3

Dewey number: 338.7'6102504252

Printed in China

Franklin Watts is a division of
Hachette Children's Books,
an Hachette UK company.

www.hachette.co.uk

DESIGN AND PRODUCTION BY **ZENO DESIGN**

PHOTOGRAPHS BY Alamy (David R. Frazier Photolibrary Inc.,
Bob Elam, Michael Gottschlak/AFP, Alex Segre, vario images
GmbH & Co.KG), Corbis (PETER MORGAN/Reuters, Kim
Kulish, Roger Ressmeyer, Ramin Talaie), Getty Images (TONY
AVELAR/AFP, FREDERIC J. BROWN/AFP, MARTIN BUREAU/
AFP, MICHAEL GOTTSCHALK/AFP, NASDAQ, Ralph Orlowski,
Panoramic Images, Mike Powell, Dick Strick/Time & Life
Pictures, Justin Sullivan)

338.7

BUILT FOR SUCCESS

THE STORY OF

Google

W
FRANKLIN WATTS
LONDON • SYDNEY

SARA GILBERT

On 19 August 2004, at 9.30am, Larry Page rang the opening bell at the **NASDAQ** Stock Market in New York City. Hours later, the 31-year-old Page and his partner, 30-year-old Sergey Brin, were multimillionaires. By the time the closing bell rang, Google, the Internet **search engine** the two friends had founded six years earlier, had sold £1 billion worth of stock in their company – and the young entrepreneurs were understandably excited. Their search engine was used by thousands of people searching for information on the World Wide Web, and had already earned a global reputation as the leader in search technology. But now Google was also a public company flush with investors' cash. And for Page and Brin, that only meant more money for more innovations.

A Stanford start

Larry Page was in Palo Alto, California, USA visiting the campus of Stanford University, which had just accepted him into its prestigious PhD programme in computer science, when he met Sergey Brin in the spring of 1995. Although Brin was only 23, a year younger than Page, he had already been in Stanford's graduate programme for two years, and was asked to help show Page around the university. Almost immediately, the two men – both bright, inquisitive and up for a good-natured argument – got on.

That friendship blossomed when Page returned to Stanford the following autumn. Almost as soon as they moved into the brand new William Gates Computer Science building – named after the chairman of the Microsoft software company, who had donated £3.8 million ($6 million) for its construction – with the rest of the computer science students and faculty, they began working together on a project to download the entire World Wide Web, and work out a way to search it using **links** as a possible **doctoral thesis**. Page had decided that the number of links pointing to a particular site was an indicator of that site's popularity and relevance. He called his system of ranking pages through links 'PageRank', a play on his own name.

Stanford University has an enrolment of more than 14,000 and a reputation as an elite university

By early 1997, PageRank had paved the way for a search engine called BackRub. Its first logo was a black-and-white scanned image of Page's left hand; when the duo decided to rename the search engine 'Google', they again opted for an inexpensive logo: the word spelt out in primary colours against a stark white background. "If you went to a design firm and asked for a home page for a search engine, you would never get that," said Stanford professor Dennis Allison. "It doesn't have any animation or metallic colours, and there is no sound or lights. It flies completely in the face of the common belief that people love to find their way through the noise."

Allison was one of many in the Stanford community who caught on to the Google phenomenon in 1997, when the search engine was made available to students, faculty and administrators at www.google.stanford.edu. Now that Brin and Page had users accessing their growing database they needed more **hardware** to store all the information they were searching. But as graduate students they had no budget for new **hard drives**. So they bought inexpensive parts, built their own machines, and hung around the loading docks on campus, looking for unclaimed computers that they could 'borrow'. They even went up to their limit on credit cards buying a huge amount of storage on disks. When they ran out of space in the office they shared with other graduate students, they turned Page's university accommodation into a data centre.

The two young men couldn't continue running their search engine on a shoestring budget. The ideal solution, they decided, was to license their search technology to an existing company. It was 1998 and the frenzy of emerging technology companies made for several potential partners. But all of the contacts they made with Internet companies such as AltaVista, Excite and Yahoo! turned into dead ends. Most companies seemed more interested in making money on advertising than in improving their search engines.

The lack of outside enthusiasm for their product only made Brin and Page more determined to improve it. They sent letters to family and friends

The Internet was expanding rapidly in the late 1990s as Larry Page and Sergey Brin built their search engine encouraging them to use the search engine and asking for suggestions on ways to improve it. They asked everyone they knew to spread the word about the site. And they constantly tweaked the way Google looked and worked, including adding short summaries for each search result so that users could immediately see which results were most relevant to them.

By late summer of 1998, Brin and Page's database included 24 million web pages – and it was still growing. But their funding was not. Then, one of their professors arranged a meeting with Andy Bechtolsheim, co-founder of Sun Microsystems and vice president of Cisco Systems, who had already made generous investments in a string of successful **start-ups**. In August 1998, Bechtolsheim met with Brin and Page, who explained what they were working on and ran a demo for him. They then discussed how they thought Google could actually make money by licensing their search technology to other Internet companies, or even selling their ideas to a large company. Bechtolsheim was impressed. "This is the single best idea I have heard in years," he said. "I want to be part of this."

His part turned out to be a $100,000 cheque, written out at once to Google, Inc – a company that, at the time, didn't even exist. Page had to tuck the cheque into his desk drawer until he and Brin had actually **incorporated** the company and opened a bank account on 7 September 1998. But for the moment, they decided to celebrate with breakfast at Burger King. Bechtolsheim, meanwhile, drove off wondering what would become of his investment. "In the back of my mind, I thought maybe they could get millions of people searching, and add it all up and make money," he said later. "I didn't know how big this could be at the time. Nobody knew."

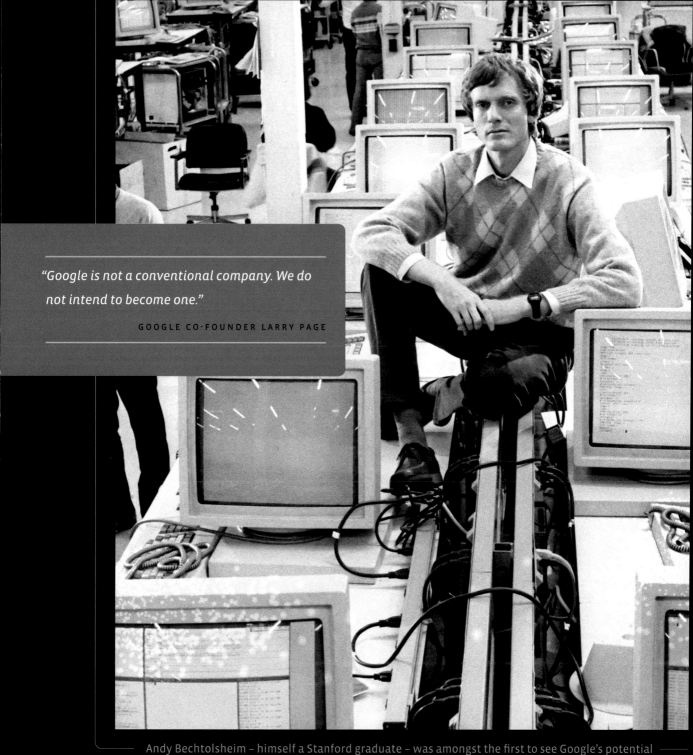

"Google is not a conventional company. We do not intend to become one."

GOOGLE CO-FOUNDER LARRY PAGE

Andy Bechtolsheim – himself a Stanford graduate – was amongst the first to see Google's potential

A NAME OF NUMBERS

Google's name is actually the result of an innocent misspelling that came out of days of brainstorming at Stanford. Larry Page and Sergey Brin had rejected idea after idea when Sean Anderson, a fellow graduate student, suggested 'googleplex' – which is actually spelt 'googolplex' and means the number 10 raised to the power googol – which represents the number 1 followed by 100 zeros. "You're trying to come up with a company that searches and indexes and allows people to organise vast amounts of data," Anderson explained. "Googleplex is a huge number." Larry Page suggested shortening it to Google, meaning the number 10 raised to the power of 100. A quick check revealed that it was still available as a domain name, so they registered the name and scrawled it on a whiteboard in the office: google.com. But the next morning, another student left a note for them: "You misspelled it. It is supposed to be G-o-o-g-o-l."

He who dares, wins

The first official Google office was in a garage in Menlo Park, California. Page and Brin, who had abandoned their studies at Stanford in 1998 to focus on their new business, rented it from a friend for £1,000 a month. They enjoyed the perks of their new site, including use of the washer and dryer and occasional dips in the hot tub at their friend's house.

But after just five months, they had outgrown the garage. In early 1999, Google and its eight employees – all working to improve the software that, by then, was handling almost 500,000 search queries a day – took up residence in an office in the centre of Palo Alto.

By then, Google.com had been mentioned in magazine articles and newspaper features, and had been named a 'Top 100 Website and Search Engine for 1998' by *PC Magazine*. It had even secured a client: Red Hat, a software firm that licensed the search technology. But it was running out of money, which was necessary to keep expanding the search technology and the company's capabilities. Page and Brin decided to seek out a **venture capital** firm for funding.

After researching their options, Page and Brin approached two of the most established firms in Silicon Valley, an area of California near San Francisco where many

This photo shows the Menlo Park garage that served as Google's headquarters in 1998 and 1999.

high-technology companies are based, hoping to secure finance from both.
The young men impressed them, not only with their technology and their long-
term plans, but also with their enthusiasm and friendly personalities. By spring
1999, both firms – Kleiner Perkins Caufield & Byers, and Sequoia Capital – were
ready to invest a total of £16 million in Google. But neither wanted to share
the investment. Brin and Page were concerned that if they accepted funds
from just one investor they would lose control over their company. Although
it was risky, they told both firms that the deal was off if they couldn't find a
way to work together.

Neither firm wanted to lose out on what looked like a promising investment.
So they decided to work together. Each company would invest £7.9 million in
Google, and each would have a seat on the company's **board of directors** – but
Page and Brin would maintain majority control. The only condition was that
the young entrepreneurs had to hire a seasoned **executive** to run the business
side of things. Page and Brin could see the value of this, and agreed.

The influx of cash allowed Google's founders to aggressively recruit top
people for their company. They had already put out feelers to their friends
in the industry, promising that new employees would get **stock options**, free
snacks and drinks at work, and the satisfaction of knowing that millions of
people were using and appreciating the software that they would have a hand
in developing. Now they could pay them as well.

But as Google hired more people and bought more computers and equipment
it inevitably ran short of space. The Palo Alto office became so cramped that
employees couldn't get up from their desks without first asking others to tuck
in their chairs. So, in late 1999, just as the tremendous interest in Internet
companies was beginning to slow down, forcing many other technology
businesses into bankruptcy, Google moved to a spacious new office in Mountain
View, California.

Located just south of San Francisco, Silicon Valley is home to many of the world's top computer businesses

As 1999 came to a close, Google was averaging a remarkable seven million searches a day – but Brin and Page still had not found a way to convert those searches into a revenue stream. Although selling advertisements was the obvious choice, they worried that allowing advertising on their site would conflict with the motto they had established for their company, hoping to differentiate it from other companies driven purely by profits: Don't Be Evil. Search results, they believed, should always be free and unaffected by advertising. But they also were beginning to see the value of selling targeted ads that could accompany search results.

The solution they agreed upon was to sell Sponsored Links, a column of text-only links that ran on the right-hand side of the results page. The advertisements, like the search results, were displayed based on relevance, using a formula that balanced how much an advertiser was willing to pay (ads were sold in an auction format, with a 'per click' price that started at 3 pence [5 cents] a click) with how many times the ad was clicked on; the more popular ads were sent to the top of the page.

By the middle of 2000, the ads had turned into a solid revenue stream for Google. But more important to Brin and Page was the announcement in June of a partnership with Yahoo! to provide the huge Internet company with search results. Not only did that relationship expand Google's online exposure by millions of computer users, it also brought a certain credibility to its product.

The same week, Google announced that its index of websites had grown to include more than a billion pages, making it the world's largest search engine – not to mention the fastest and most relevant. "Now you can search the equivalent of a stack of paper more than 70 miles (113 kilometres) high in less than half a second," Page said. "We think that's pretty cool."

"Don't be afraid of failure. The more you stumble around, the more likely you are to stumble across something valuable. And go into computer science only if you love it, not for the money."

GOOGLE CO-FOUNDER SERGEY BRIN'S ADVICE TO STUDENTS

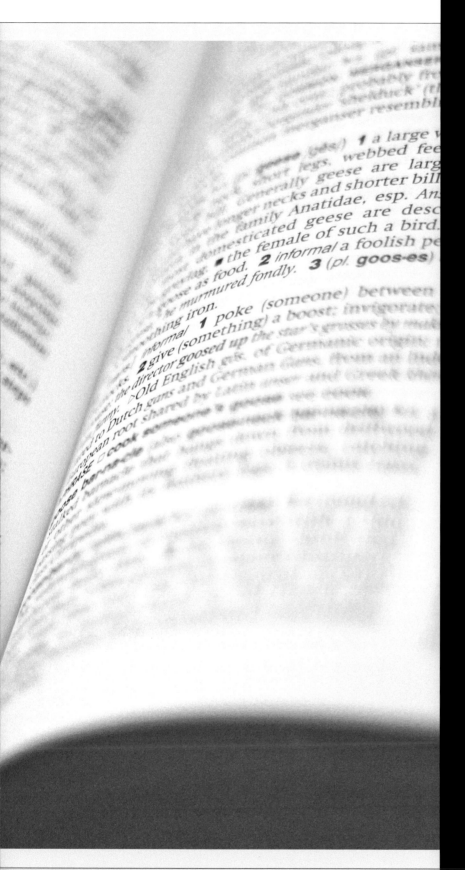

GOOGLE (VERB)

Google's founders never considered their company's name anything more than a noun meaning a very large number and representing the enormous size of their indexes. But users of the search engine quickly turned the name into a verb: people 'googled' restaurants, schools and even classmates, prospective employers and dates. In 2006, a pair of dictionary publishers made that transition official. US dictionary *Merriam-Webster* defined 'google' as a transitive verb meaning to use the Google search engine "to obtain information about (a person) on the World Wide Web". Likewise, the *Oxford English Dictionary* included it as a verb, but listed it as 'Google' capitalised. "A noun turns into a verb very often," explained Thomas Pitoniak, the associate editor and composition manager for *Merriam-Webster*. "Google is a unique case. Because they have achieved so much prominence in the world of search, people have been using the word google as a generic verb now."

Google grows

In less than three years, Google had experienced incredible growth. By the start of 2001, it was handling more than 100 million search queries a day. And it had set out to make those searches better and more convenient by establishing relationships with several wireless Internet providers, to make its technology available over mobile phones and other devices. By the fourth **quarter**, it had recorded its first annual profit of £4.4 million.

But Page and Brin were negligent in carrying out a promise they had made to their investors: they had not yet hired a chief executive officer (CEO) to run the business. Although John Doerr, a partner with the investment firm Kleiner Perkins, had arranged for several candidates to meet with them, the Google founders had seen reasons to reject all of them. When Eric Schmidt, a former chief technology officer for Sun Microsystems, came to Google's offices in late 2000, they expected to reject him as well. Schmidt, who was in the process of co-ordinating a **merger** for his new company, software maker Novell, wasn't very much interested in their search engine or their job offer. But the meeting surprised both parties.

Starting around the year 2000, Google focused on making its technology available on wireless devices.

The Google men took Schmidt to task for some of his strategy decisions at Novell. Schmidt argued back. It was exactly the kind of intellectual duel that Brin and Page thrived on. By the time Schmidt left, the founders realised that they actually liked him. They called him later to discuss his interest in the company and their interest in him. "We don't need you now," Page said, "but we think we're going to need you in the future."

The future came quickly. In August 2001, Schmidt became CEO and chairman of the company. His job would be to play the role of disciplinarian in Google's young, creative environment. He was amazed to find that the company was still using small business software solutions for financial accounting and payroll systems, and quickly implemented a system better suited to a company making millions of dollars.

Occasionally, Schmidt's business sense conflicted with the ambitions of Brin and Page – most notably when the pair was on the verge of sealing a deal as the official search engine of Internet giant America Online (AOL). AOL was asking for a huge financial guarantee from Google, as well as stock options. Although Brin and Page were willing to pay any price for the business, Schmidt wanted them to approach the deal more conservatively. The founders pulled rank on their CEO, however, and confidently completed the deal.

On 1 May 2002, AOL's 34 million subscribers found a small search box on every page that said 'Search Powered by Google'. Soon, Google had also signed a deal to provide searches for Internet provider Earthlink. Next came a three-year, £63-million deal to provide rival search engine Ask Jeeves with its text-based advertising. By the end of 2002, Google's balance sheet reflected £277 million in sales and £63 million in profits. Schmidt admitted that Brin and Page had been right to pursue those partnerships. "They were more willing to take risks than me," he said. "They turned out to be right."

Brin and Page put much of the money that was coming in back into innovative ideas for expanding the search business – many of which came

An experienced corporate leader, Eric Schmidt helped Google take off in earnest after being hired as CEO in 2001

from the company's own employees. Google News, which offered free access to more than 4,500 news sources worldwide, was launched in September 2002. Froogle, a product search service, went online in test mode for the holiday shopping season a few months later. Google went global by making the site searchable in hundreds of languages, from Greek and Chinese to Russian and Danish, and even a few 'just for fun' tongues: pig Latin and Klingon, for example.

As Google's product was improving, its appeal to advertisers was growing. So was its AdSense programme, which offered other websites the technology to generate revenue by selling targeted ads that could be placed adjacent to their content. Of course, each site that bought the technology sent money to Google. The company was growing so fast and gaining so much positive attention that it had caught the eye of software giant Microsoft, which was reeling from a lawsuit claiming it had sought to establish a monopoly with its computer operating system. Google's success made Microsoft nervous about losing its position of dominance in the software industry. Although the two companies didn't compete head-to-head, they would both try to outdo the other with innovations and new ideas from that point onwards.

As 2003 came to an end, Google's site index had grown to include 4.28 billion web pages. The company was being lauded in the press – it had been called 'Brand of the Year' by Brandchannel, while Page and Brin had been called 'Persons of the Week' by ABC News [major US television network show] – and also praised by users. As the company celebrated its fifth birthday, it seemed that things couldn't possibly get any better.

WHO'S BEHIND THE CARTOON MAYHEM? ■ BEING OBAMA

TIME

RUST

gle

Google honchos,
from top,
Larry Page,
Eric Schmidt and
Sergey Brin

SECRETS?

An exclusive inside look
at the $100 billion empire
that is dominating
the Internet

BY ADI IGNATIUS

"Google's growth shows no sign of slowing.
Despite capturing the majority of searches
in the US, and in light of competitors'
improvements, Google's market share of
executed searches continues to grow…"

BILL TANCER, RESEARCH MANAGER AT
HITWISE, AN INTERNET METRICS FIRM

By 2003, Google's 'big three' of Page, Brin and Schmidt were being featured in major journals

Every week, the software engineers at Google are encouraged to set aside their pressing projects for one day and focus on creative ideas of their own instead. It's known as the 20 per cent rule – and it's helped launch several of Google's best-known products and services. Google News, for example, came out of an employee's efforts to organise news reports in the aftermath of the 9/11 terror attacks; Froogle, Google's shopping site, was developed by an engineer who spent his 20 per cent time studying product searches. Another engineer created 'Google 101', a seminar to better prepare students for computer careers. Even Gmail, Google's free webmail service, came out of a 20 per cent time project. Not every 20 per cent time project comes to fruition, but CEO Eric Schmidt says the company relies on the ideas for innovation. "Virtually everything new seems to come from the 20 per cent time," Schmidt says. "They certainly don't come from the management team."

Searching the stock market

Although business was booming in 2004, Larry Page and Sergey Brin were convinced that they could do better. In particular, they were convinced that they could do email better than such competitors as Microsoft, Yahoo! and America Online. They wanted their version to be cheaper, easier to use and superior in every other way to competing brands.

On 1 April 2004, when Page and Brin announced the launch of Gmail with a press release they expected a lot of buzz. They were, after all, offering a greater amount of online storage space – a full **gigabyte** – to all subscribers, which was still unheard of in the industry. Even better, there was no cost at all for users. But the excitement that came out of their announcement was focused almost entirely on an aspect to which they hadn't given much thought: the fact that Google intended to run targeted adverts in the emails. Privacy advocates were furious that the content of emails sent and received would be scanned to find keywords that could be paired with ads. Lawmakers threatened legislation. For the first time, Google's 'golden boy' image had been tarnished in a very public way.

"Google is risking its reputation for honesty and putting the user first with its new email service," wrote Walt Mossberg, a technology columnist for the *Wall Street*

Like Google, Yahoo! was founded by two Stanford graduate students (Jerry Yang and David Filo)

Journal. "The problem here isn't confusion between ads and editorial content. It's that Google is scanning your private email to locate the keywords that generate the ads. This seems like an invasion of privacy."

Brin and Page were completely unprepared for the negative reaction to their Gmail announcement. They were convinced that the storm would blow over once users had a chance to experience the product, but they still consulted a lawyer, who advised them to take steps to make searching email archives impossible and to strip personal information about users from their records. They did not, however, change their plans to run ads with the emails.

The furore over Gmail was still raging when, on 29 April 2004, Google filed with the Securities and Exchange Commission (SEC) for an **initial public offering** (IPO). Although Page and Brin were not eager to give up the freedom of private ownership, they knew it was time to reward the employees they had recruited with promises of stock options. They also knew that their investors – from the venture capital firms and Andy Bechtolsheim, to the friends and family who had helped raise early funds – deserved to cash in on their investments. And they knew that an infusion of cash would allow their company to maintain its growth and achieve new things. But, as usual, it wasn't their style to go about the process in the conventional manner.

Their first move was to set the amount of money they hoped to raise through the IPO at $2,718,281,828.46 (£1,712,517,551.93) – a numerical figure known as 'constant e'. They also refused to limit the number of investment houses guaranteeing the sale of stock, which most companies do. Then they decided to set the price of Google's shares through an unusual and relatively unknown Dutch auction process, which allowed investors to bid for the shares online.

In the months between that announcement and the actual IPO, Google again faced fire from the media, industry analysts and Wall Street observers, who thought the company was pricing its stock too high (the original forecast was for a range between £68 and £85 a share), and that it was being careless with

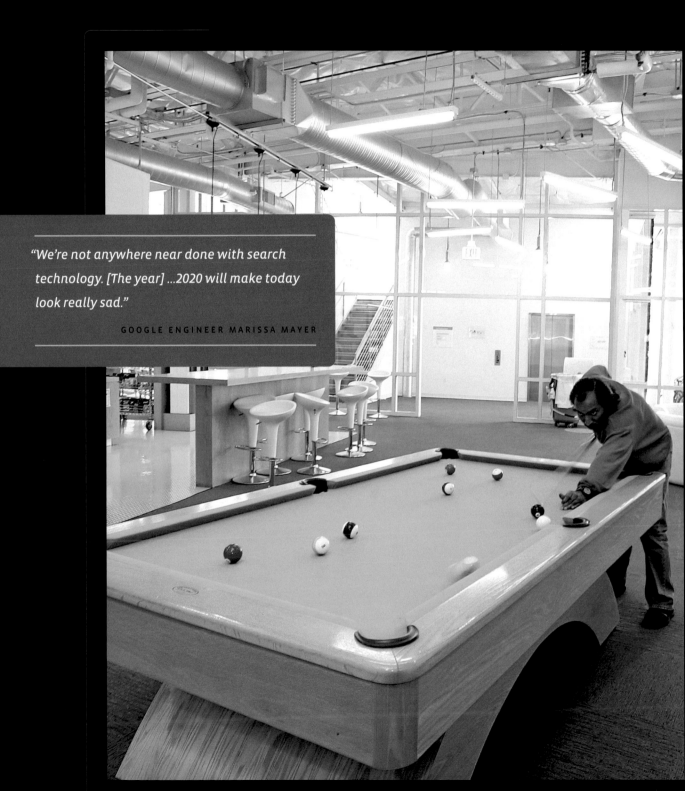

"We're not anywhere near done with search technology. [The year] ...2020 will make today look really sad."

GOOGLE ENGINEER MARISSA MAYER

Google's comfortable offices in Mountain View, California were designed to encourage creativity the rules for stock offerings. Some traditional business people even considered Brin and Page to be arrogant and immature because they were doing things in a non-standard way.

But the worst was yet to come. During what is known as 'the quiet period', in which the SEC requires a company issuing stock to refrain from any promotional publicity, Page and Brin were featured in a lengthy article in *Playboy* magazine. The interview had taken place in early April, before the company had even announced that it would be going public. The timing of its publication, however, was problematic. But Google's lawyers offered a possible solution: file the *Playboy* article as an **appendix** to the company's SEC registration statement, making it part of the official materials available to all investors. The plan worked. Although the SEC reserved the right to investigate the matter further at a later date, it allowed the IPO to go forward.

All the attention came to a head on 19 August 2004, when Google began trading on NASDAQ for £54 a share. Page went to Wall Street for the occasion, but Brin stayed in California to shepherd the company's day-to-day operations. By the end of the day, both men were multimillionaires. Their company had raised £1 billion – short of their expectations, but still amongst the largest totals ever raised by a technology company.

In the wake of Google's IPO, Sergey Brin, Larry Page and CEO Eric Schmidt all offered to take pay cuts. Brin and Page had been earning £95,000 annually, and Schmidt £157,000. But after each took home millions of dollars from the stock offering they reduced their salaries to 63p ($1) a year.

Google's IPO in August 2004 instantly turned many of the company's employees into millionaires

A GOOGLER'S WORKDAY

Free food. A swimming pool, climbing wall and pool tables. Laundry facilities (with free washing powder) on-site. That's just the beginning of the benefits Google offers to its more than 6,500 employees, from software engineers to secretaries. There's also the on-site beauty salon, doctor's surgery and spa (all free). Working parents can bring their children to the free crèche at the company's headquarters in Mountain View, California. Dogs are welcome. Employees are even given access to motorised scooters to travel around the sprawling Googleplex. And every so often it's pyjama day. Co-founders Larry Page and Sergey Brin have gone to such lengths to keep their employees happy that their company was called the 'Best Company to Work For' by *Fortune Magazine* in 2007. "Work is such a cosy place that it's sometimes difficult for Google employees to leave the office," writer Adam Lashinsky said in the article "which is precisely how the company justifies the expenses."

Engines roaring

Google held its first annual meeting for **shareholders** on 12 May 2005. The few hundred who attended at the Googleplex (the company headquarters) for the meeting were treated to lunch, followed by 'snicker-Google' cookies, the company's spin on snickerdoodles [cinnamon biscuits].

Although they didn't get a tour of the headquarters – any attendee could have been from a competitor – they did get good news: the company's stock had soared past £141. Profits for the first three months of the year were at £232.7 million, with sales topping £0.8 billion. By American Independence Day (4 July), Google's stock exceeded £190, an unprecedented high for technology stock.

The good news continued all year long, as Google developed new products such as Google Maps, a directions and locations search, and Google Earth, which allowed users to view satellite images, maps and three-dimensional images of sites around the world, down to buildings, objects such as cars – and sometimes even people. The company also expanded internationally, extending its agreement with America Online to provide search and advertising technology to AOL Europe, gaining exposure to approximately 6.3 million

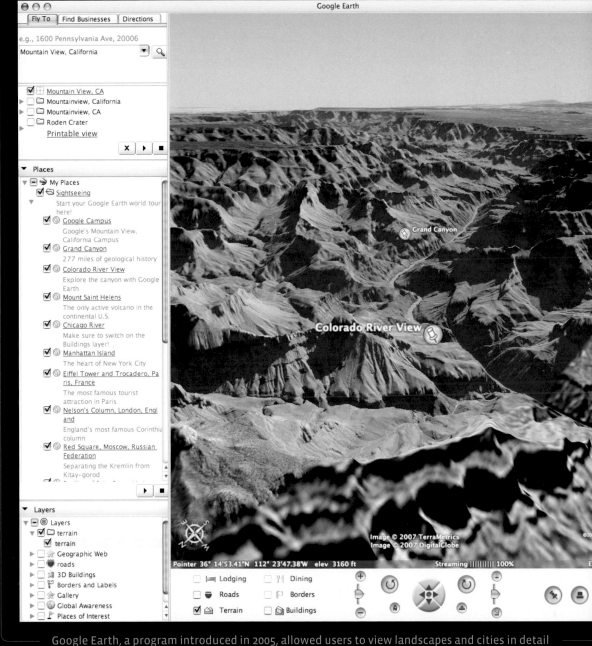

Google Earth, a program introduced in 2005, allowed users to view landscapes and cities in detail

GOOGLE

people. It opened a European headquarters in Dublin, Ireland, a research and development centre in Beijing, China, and offices in both Sao Paulo, Brazil and Mexico City, Mexico.

Near the end of the year, Google renamed one of its most ambitious projects to date: Google Print became Google Book Search, a collection of online books from some of the world's largest and most prestigious libraries that had been scanned as part of Google's digitisation project. The project had started in 2002, when Page approached his alma mater, the University of Michigan, with an offer to pay to have every book in the school's library scanned if he could add all the information to Google's index. He and Brin floated similar proposals at Stanford, Harvard, the New York Public Library and others.

Even as they made those offers, they had no idea how long it would take to photograph each page so that it could be digitally scanned. Page and Marissa Mayer, Google's director of consumer web products, started experimenting with the process. "We had a metronome to keep us on rhythm for turning the pages," Mayer said. "Larry's job was to click the shutter, and my job was to turn the pages. It took us about 45 minutes to do a 300-page book."

This was encouraging enough for the Google team to continue. Although the idea drew controversy over **copyright infringement** from some author groups, the company was willing to commit time and resources over the long term to the ongoing digitisation project. "Maybe inside of 10 years we'll have all the knowledge that's ever been published in book form available and searchable online," Mayer said. "It's really a grand vision."

Google pursued the ideas of others almost as eagerly as it pursued its own. The company had already made several key acquisitions in its short history, each one adding another dimension to its own offerings. It bought Pyra Labs, which brought a **blogging** presence to Google. It acquired Upstartle, which brought an online word processing and spreadsheet component to the business. And in October 2006, Google paid £1.04 billion in stock to buy YouTube, a popular

By 2007, Google Book Search included more than a million digitised books, and was scanning another 3,000 a day online video site. "The YouTube team has built an exciting and powerful media platform that complements Google's mission to organise the world's information and make it universally accessible and useful," said Eric Schmidt. "Our companies share similar values; we both always put our users first, and are committed to innovating to improve their experience."

Google was growing bigger and bigger – and its renown was reaching further and further. By the end of 2006, it was far and away the most used search engine on the Web, with a **market share** of more than 50 per cent. Its closest competitor, Yahoo!, which had at one time used Google technology, claimed just 23 per cent. The company's name had become synonymous with 'search', and had been added to the dictionary as a verb.

Such dominance led industry experts to wonder if another company could ever surpass Google as the leader in search technology. "It's inevitable," said Erik Hansen, president of SiteSpect, a provider of search engine marketing and web optimisation technology, in 2007. "Google cannot stay on top forever. Yes, it is in the spotlight now, but a lot of smart and well-funded companies are developing technology that is different from what Google offers."

Such speculation only pushes the 'googlers' at the Googleplex to work towards the next best thing – from searching television services and offering on-air advertising plans, to voice-activated telephone directory searches, mobile phone services and any number of other, as yet undisclosed plans. "We don't talk much about what lies ahead," the company reported on its website, "because we believe one of our chief competitive advantages is surprise."

In a very short time, Google has offered its users one surprise after another. The company may have been founded on a dream and a shoestring budget, but in under 10 years, it has become one of the most profitable businesses in the world. Considering the dedication of Google's two young founders, this isn't such a surprise. "I think we all feel a tremendous amount of responsibility for getting many, many people in the world their information," Larry Page said.

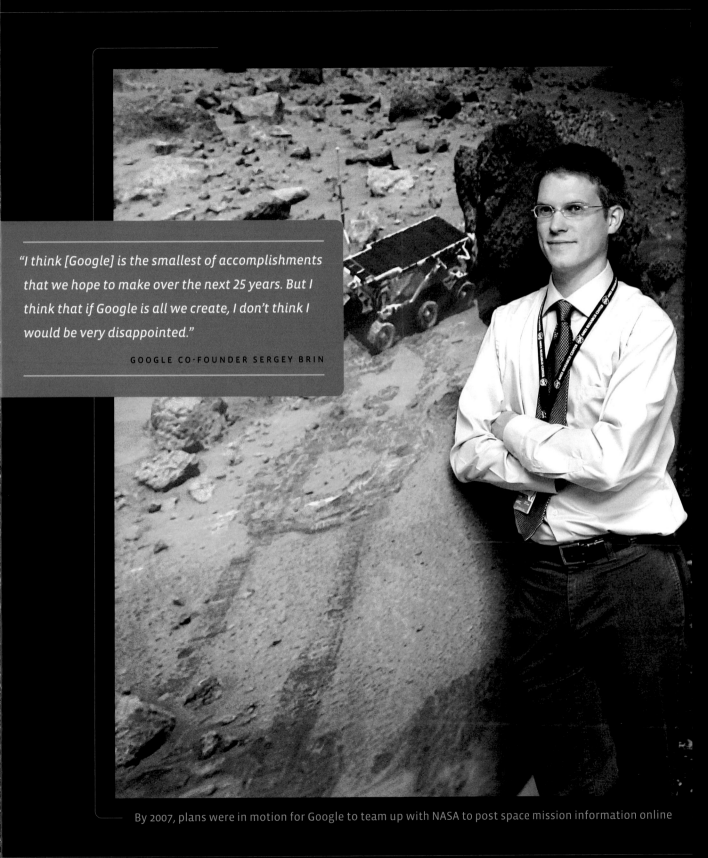

"I think [Google] is the smallest of accomplishments that we hope to make over the next 25 years. But I think that if Google is all we create, I don't think I would be very disappointed."

GOOGLE CO-FOUNDER SERGEY BRIN

By 2007, plans were in motion for Google to team up with NASA to post space mission information online

Company lore insists that Larry Page and Sergey Brin didn't particularly like each other when they met as PhD students on the Stanford campus in 1995. They were known to challenge each other constantly and to argue, often over silly ideas (including, as one fellow student recalled, whether it was possible to construct a building-size display out of lima [butter] beans). But the two have been nearly inseparable since that time. They were so frequently seen together on campus that their names eventually became one – 'LarryandSergey'. Soon, so did their academic pursuits. By mid-1996, Page and Brin, who shared office space in Stanford's William Gates Science Center, were working together to download and analyse web links. Two years later, they had turned that idea into the Google search engine. Today they continue to be almost constant companions – and they still share an office (albeit a much more spacious one) at the sprawling Googleplex.

Larry Page (left) and Sergey Brin

GLOSSARY

appendix a collection of supplementary material that is attached to documentation to help explain or clarify other materials

blogging contributing regularly to an ongoing personal journal about a specified topic on the World Wide Web

board of directors a group of people in charge of making big decisions for a company

copyright infringement a violation of rights in which one person or company benefits by using the work or ideas of another person or company illegally

doctoral thesis a written paper based on research examining a new idea or point of view, especially as a requirement for an advanced academic degree

executive a decision-making leader of a company, such as the president or chief executive officer (CEO)

gigabyte a unit of computer memory or data storage capacity equal to 1,024 megabytes, or one billion bytes (computer hard drives often have 160 or more gigabytes)

hard drives computer parts that read and write data, or information, on computer disks

hardware computers and associated physical equipment directly involved in processing data

incorporated forming a firm or company into a corporation by completing all of the required procedures and paperwork

initial public offering the first sale of stock by a company to the public; it is generally done to raise funds for the company, which is then owned by investors rather than an individual or group of individuals

links a segment of text or a graphical item that serves as a cross-reference between parts of a Web-based document or between different web pages

market share the percentage of the total sales of a given type of product or service that is attributable to a particular company

merger the combining of two or more entities into one through a purchase or a pooling of interests

NASDAQ an acronym for the National Association of Securities Dealers Automated Quotation system; it is a computerised system used to trade shares in public companies

quarter one of four three-month intervals that together comprise the financial year; public companies must report certain data on a quarterly basis

search engine a website whose primary function is locating information available on the Internet or a portion of the Internet

shareholders people or corporations who own shares of stock (portions of ownership) in a corporation

start-ups new business ventures in their earliest stage of development

stock options options for employees or investors in a company to buy or sell that company's stock; stock options are often given as part of an employee's benefits package

venture capital funds made available to small businesses that are starting out, but that show great potential for growth

TIMELINE

1995	Larry Page and Sergey Brin meet at Stanford University and start PageRank
1997	PageRank changes to Google. The search engine becomes available for all at Stanford University
1998	Google includes 24 million web pages and Andy Bechtolsheim invests in the company
1999	Kleiner Perkins Caufield & Beyers and Sequoia Capital both invest £7.9 million into Google
2000	Google and Yahoo! partnership
2001	Eric Schmidt becomes CEO and chairman
2002	Google News is launched
2004	Google's own email system, Gmail, made available. Google begins trading shares on NASDAQ
2005	First official shareholders meeting
2006	The word "google' is added into the Merriam-Webster and Oxford English Dictionary. Google buys YouTube
2007	Named 'Best Company to Work For' by Fortune Magazine

INDEX